FACE
FEAR
&
LIVE

FACE FEAR & LIVE

Twelve Steps to Heal from What Hurt You

TRACY EVANSON

TRACY'S
HEALING
ROOM

ByThe | Designed by Anna Perotti
Book |
Design | bythebookdesign.com

ISBN 979-8-9954022-0-6

Printed in the United States of America

CONTENTS

This book exists because of the people who

walked with me while I learned how to heal.

To those who choose to heal, even when it's

hard, and to those who want to heal but don't

yet know where to start, this work is for you.

AUTHOR'S LETTER

Before we ever make a decision, before we choose a relationship, before we learn how to say yes or no, we are asking two questions from within: Who am I? Am I worthy of being loved as I am? Identity shapes everything, and I struggled with those questions and concepts from the very beginning.

Growing up, I was a biracial child in a predominantly Hispanic and Latin community. Even in my earliest memories, I perceived myself as different—present, but not fully belonging. I didn't have the understanding of identity then, but I felt its absence. When you don't know who you are, you are vulnerable to becoming who others need you to be. When your identity feels unclear, approval and validation start to feel like a matter of survival because we're looking to others to tell us who we are.

Abandonment only compounded my confusion about who I was. My father left while my mother was pregnant with me, so as I got older, I was left to internalize that absence in the only way a child could: If he left, something must be wrong with me. So, alongside wondering who I was, another wound came along: Why wasn't I loved enough for him to stay? Those questions don't disappear with age. They follow you.

During my childhood, I experienced what many minimize as just "kid" stuff: name-calling, insults about my physical appearance (specifically regarding my hair, nose, and body), and the use of racial slurs. But when you are already struggling to understand who you are, those moments don't bounce off you. They land. They stack. They chip away at something that hasn't had the chance to solidify yet. Eventually, I did find acceptance, though, by other kids who lived on my block. One family even welcomed me as one of their own. They had four children already, and still, there was always room for me at the table. I felt safe there. Comfortable. At home. But when acceptance comes before you have learned to accept yourself, the relief is without roots. Without realizing it, I began adapting, absorbing their identity, their values, and their way of being; not because these characteristics fully fit me, but because I was searching. Scraping. Trying desperately to belong somewhere.

Even though many children and adults strive to "fit in," I don't believe that is the true thing they're after. I believe people want to belong—to be seen, chosen, and valued for what they bring—and I didn't feel valuable from the start. So, even when I found a few kids from my neighborhood who I "fit in" with, it didn't fill the cracks I felt inside.

Then, when I was five, a neighbor violated me. That experience didn't just take something from me; it confirmed a belief I was already forming: My boundaries don't matter, and my body isn't fully mine. It also showed me that attention, even harmful attention, was still a form of being seen. This was just the beginning of me drifting further away from myself. Shortly after that, before I even had a chance to fully understand the first incident, another moment imprinted itself on me. In first grade, a teacher asked me to retrieve something from her office, but I couldn't find it. When I returned to tell her that, she grabbed me by my hair and dragged me back to the classroom. I can't recall whether the item was actually missing or if I overlooked it, but I do remember the fear I felt. That moment taught me another lesson long before I had words for it: Disappointing people is dangerous. At only five years old, I learned that adults had power over me and that my safety depended on compliance. I learned that being small meant not having choices, and that resistance wasn't something I yet knew how to access. So, when the incident with my first-grade teacher happened, the fear felt familiar. Different moment. Same lesson.

Reflecting, I don't remember being told to stay quiet about how they treated me. I don't remember warnings or instructions or words at all, but from that point on, I became deeply afraid of getting in trouble by doing things incorrectly or saying no. I learned to please others at the cost of myself. I learned to abandon my own needs to feel safe. Those patterns didn't come from weakness; they came from adaptation. And as I got older, they followed me into relationships and friendships. I was the girl everyone confided in. The one who held secrets. The matchmaker. The emotional caretaker. I was rarely the one chosen—but I was always nearby as a backup. So, when someone wanted my attention, my body, or my time, it felt like enough. I mistook being wanted for being valued.

At thirteen, I entered my first relationship. He wasn't cruel or abusive, but he was going down a bad path—and I followed. He drank, so I drank. He used drugs, so I used drugs. He skipped school, so I skipped school. Doing these things together felt like connection, and I was just grateful to feel chosen. Then, a close friend of mine from this inner circle became pregnant, and overnight, everything around us changed. The bad behaviors stopped, but not because of sudden clarity, the need for discipline, or because I had figured things out. It was much simpler than that: The environment that had encouraged these decisions in the first place fell away. Without realizing it, I stepped off that path. I knew what I had been doing wasn't right, but as I searched for a sense of belonging, I found myself willing to compromise myself in the process. So, when that sense of belonging disappeared, so did the momentum. But even though I shifted course, the underlying wounds remained.

Entering my high school years, I was still trying to embrace the parts of myself that I could not change, but for some reason, I consistently developed feelings for boys whose families did not accept me. I remember meeting one boy's mother and, thinking I couldn't understand Spanish, heard her say, "Está fea." (She's ugly). I carried that moment, pretending acceptance where there was rejection. But because I subconsciously looked to people for self-acceptance and a sense of value, these experiences led me to continue to want to change everything about myself. My nose. My body. A mole on my lip that kids mocked. Each comment reinforced the belief that I was the problem and that fixing myself was the solution.

I want to be clear: Abuse does not discriminate. It can happen to any child. The ones with a safe childhood, smart ones who do well in class, ones who love how they look, and ones who are great at sports. But for any of those children, this level of low self-esteem becomes dangerous. Predators look for uncertainty. In my case, my lack of self-worth made it easier for someone to believe their tactics would work on me, not because I was weak, but because emotional language and coping tools weren't given to me to navigate those scenarios. I realize that the people who raised me were doing the best they could with what they knew, though. They had survived their own hardships, and they passed down what had helped them endure: figure it out, toughen up, and don't let them get to you. Even at times, forget them and move on. That mindset was their survival, and it worked. But it didn't teach me how to pour into myself. It didn't teach me how to name my feelings, protect my boundaries, or build self-worth from the inside out. Instead, it taught me how to brace for impact. What I needed were tools for self-understanding, confidence, and care that no one in my life had ever been given themselves.

At my core, I am a lover, not a fighter. Even when I was younger, I didn't want my experiences to make me hard, and I most definitely didn't want to become someone who struck back. I just wanted to remove myself from harm, keeping what remained of me close. But I didn't yet know how to do that. And that is why I wrote this book—because I don't want anyone else to spend decades untangling these wounds alone.

I wrote Face Fear and Live for those who feel behind before they've even begun. For those who learned to adapt instead of develop. For those who became whoever they needed to be to survive, and then lost themselves along the way. My journey to myself has taken years and is full of heartbreak, courage, reckoning, and grace. And now, I am deeply in love with who I am—not because I am perfect, but because I am whole. This book, my story, is an invitation for anyone who feels as if they're missing a vital piece of who they are and is ready to begin that journey for themselves. All it takes is intention and the true belief that happiness and peace are waiting for them.

INTRODUCTION

Everyone has an idea of what family is supposed to look like, what love should feel like, and what safety, belonging, and connection are meant to be. Often, those ideas are shaped not by what we're told, but by what we see.

I was not raised in a two-parent home. Instead, I was raised by a strong single mother and a devoted grandmother. They loved me profoundly. They cared for me. They protected me. But outside of my family, I grew up surrounded by other kids who appeared whole. Two parents. Stability. A sense of togetherness that felt natural and assumed. I wanted that. I longed for it. I cried for it. I believed that if I could just have that kind of family, everything would feel right. I wouldn't have to constantly wonder why my dad didn't want me.

Children don't have the ability to rationalize adult circumstances. It doesn't matter how capable or loving their parent is. No child wants to be raised by one parent, and no explanation of why they are will help. They simply notice who is missing, and they internalize it. It took me a long time to comprehend this, too. As I transitioned from childhood into adolescence, I had come to accept my family dynamic, not even realizing I was "less fortunate." I had my mom, the influence of a supportive grandmother, and the presence of an uncle who offered male guidance when he could. Everything that was poured into me came from hearts that gave their very best, and there was never a time I felt unloved by them. I will be forever grateful for the love I received from those beautiful souls. But adolescence has a way of stirring questions that were once quiet.

At thirteen years old, an already tender and confusing age, my absent father reached out for the first time. It was a phone call, and I was the one who answered. The man on the line asked for my mom, so I passed her the phone. She greeted whoever it was and then said, "What is this? Some kind of joke?" Confused, I watched as she walked out of the living room and into her bedroom to have a private conversation. She came back a few minutes later and said, "Your father wants to meet you." I was ecstatic. Hope flooded in instantly. I was finally going to meet the man I had wondered about my entire life. I knew nothing about this man other than that he was white and a construction worker. No pictures. No stories. No access. But now, I was finally going to get the missing pieces to the puzzle. My mom seemed like she was in a state of shock and disbelief, but I was only focused on how happy I felt. When it was getting close to the time I'd meet him, I remember being overly concerned about my appearance. I wanted to make sure I looked pretty. I wanted my hair done and the right outfit. After all, worth was tied to physical appearance back then.

That summer day in 1985, he came to my home. He gave me a card with a single rose. The front of the card read, "There is something I've been wanting to say to you for a long time." When I opened it, it simply said, "Hello." In that moment, I was the happiest thirteen-year-old girl in the world.

Unfortunately, that feeling didn't last.

After the initial excitement wore off, I started wondering why it took thirteen years for him to acknowledge me. I didn't understand adult prejudice, racial tension, or family dynamics rooted in belief systems that existed long before I did. My mother is Black, and my father is White—a reality that shaped how their relationship was received and how my absence from his life was decided. In addition to that, I later learned that my father was living quite a turbulent lifestyle and wasn't ready for a child. But that is not how a child processes abandonment. Instead, a child asks one question over and over again, silently and subconsciously: What is wrong with me? And I brought that inner turmoil into my new relationship with him. Looking back now, I can trace the beginning of my acting-out behaviors to that year—starting with dating that boy who was going nowhere. That turned into drinking, smoking, doing drugs, cutting school, and promiscuity. I was trying to make sense of something far bigger than my emotional capacity could hold.

Over the next several years, I attempted to navigate a relationship with my father and his family. They welcomed me and treated me kindly, but my feelings of anger, grief, confusion, and not having any control over when he left or when he returned eventually became too heavy. So, at eighteen, I walked away. Doing this felt like the only control over my life I had left.

It wasn't until I was twenty-three, after giving birth to my first child, that I reconsidered that decision. It felt unfair to deny my daughter the opportunity to get to know her grandfather because of my unresolved pain. So, I reached out again, and as before, my father was happy and just as welcoming. His family was still kind to me, inviting me to holidays, family dinners, and shared spaces that should have felt like home. And yet, something was missing. No matter how much I wanted to, I didn't feel that unbreakable bond. Instead, I felt like a visiting guest—polite, grateful, careful. I showed up as the most proper version of myself, not the most authentic one. But even so, we all continued the effort of trying to make up for lost time.

As I prepared for my first marriage and planned my wedding, my father and stepmother were deeply supportive, monetarily and emotionally, which is something I appreciate, even with the feelings of disconnect at times. My stepmom stepped into the role as wedding planner while my dad prepared my mom's backyard for our ceremony with some needed construction. Their effort and care were genuine and generous, making for a beautiful, picture-perfect wedding. This celebration of love made me feel as if a clean slate could actually be possible, but that hope didn't last. Our daughter was just one year old when we got married, and within two years, that marriage ended. Shortly after, I entered another relationship—one that became abusive for nearly a decade. I had two more children during that time, and eventually, I escaped for all of our well-being. However, by then, I had learned how to endure distance without naming it, so for those ten years, my relationship with my father remained cordial but cautious, distantly present, existing in form, but rarely in proximity and never in depth.

By my mid-thirties, I had faced parent abandonment, family racism, childhood sexual abuse, teenage promiscuity, a failed marriage, and a prolonged abusive relationship. I was a single mother of three—exhausted, overwhelmed, buried in debt, carrying low self-worth, and quietly ashamed of the life I believed I had created. I had become the very family structure I once swore I would never repeat. And that realization broke me. However, it was in being broken that I finally saw the pieces I needed to put my life back together. The next ten years became a season of rebuilding, both externally and internally. I made a decision to heal. To develop. To grow. Three little humans depended on me, and there was a version of my childhood self inside of me who deserved healing, too.

I grew up in the church, but what I knew then was religion, not relationship. Faith was something we attended, not something we talked about. My mother would drop me off at Sunday school and pick me up when it was over, but God was never a presence I felt connected to or understood personally. Years later, during a season when I was struggling and searching for something to hold onto, a friend invited me to attend church with her. Feeling lost and out of options, I agreed. I was desperate to be happy, desperate for relief, and unsure of what else to do. What I found there wasn't instant healing, but support, direction, and a sense that I didn't have to carry everything alone. That was when I fully surrendered to my Lord and Savior, Jesus Christ, with a commitment to heal with intention. I pursued growth relentlessly, emotionally, spiritually, and intellectually. I returned to school. I invested in my development. I surrounded myself with people who reflected where I was going, not where I had been.

I learned something transformative along the way: Bad things happening to me did not mean I deserved them, and they did not diminish my worth. This is when I came to realize that I was never broken. I was only wounded, and wounds can heal. After I came to accept this new perspective, I saw that I had the power to rewrite the narrative I had been telling myself for years—that I was unwanted, unlovable, and not enough. But it takes more than just seeing the truth to heal. Healing follows a process.

And this book is that process.

Face Fear and Live is a twelve-step journey designed to help you heal from what hurt you, not by erasing the past, but by reframing it. By forgiving. Accepting. Becoming courageous. Eliminating what no longer serves you. Choosing freedom. Empowering yourself. Affirming truth. Renewing your mind. Loving fully. Inspiring others. Honoring your value. And ultimately, edifying the world around you.

You are not alone in this journey.

And what happened to you does not define you.

OI

HEALING
THE
FOUNDATION

I LEARNED
TO FORGIVE
OTHERS, NOT
BECAUSE THEY
DESERVED IT,
BUT BECAUSE
I DESERVED
PEACE.

1

FORGIVE

It's Not for Them: It's for You

I didn't realize how much unforgiveness was shaping my life. For years, I was just trying to survive, day after day, decision after decision. I didn't wake up thinking: I'm unforgiving. Instead, the first thought I had in the morning was: I need to get through today. I didn't recognize that the anger I carried, toward my father, my first marriage, and my ex, was quietly influencing every aspect of my life. At the time, I didn't see my unforgiveness as bitterness. I saw it as protection. It took a long time before I realized it was that very same unforgiveness that was holding me back.

My father hurt me by leaving. My first marriage hurt me because I never felt truly chosen, like I was forcing someone to love me. The father of my two youngest children hurt me through years of abuse. These were the relationships in my life that built my definition of what male love was. So, over time, I began to believe that love was something I had to chase, earn, or prove I was deserving of it. And when people didn't choose me, I told myself I didn't need them, that I didn't care. I built a hard exterior, convincing myself I was better off alone. But subconsciously, the very pain I claimed didn't affect me, consumed my heart. Many people assume that when you hold on to unforgiveness, it only shows up as rage, but that's not the case. Sometimes, the signs are more subtle than that, showing up as distance, self-sabotage, and walls disguised as strength. I believed everyone was eventually going to hurt me, so I made excuses for not getting close to people. I stayed guarded, closed off, and suspicious, not realizing that unforgiveness was blocking my ability to receive love.

And the most dangerous part? I didn't even know it.

I developed negative coping mechanisms, and even though I had three children who I desperately wanted to be a good role model for, I made choices I wasn't proud of when they were asleep or gone for the weekend—choices they would never have been proud of either. I drank too much, I involved myself with people I had no business being involved with, and I put myself in compromising situations. I did these things again and again, and each time, I felt worse about myself. Each time, the shame deepened. And yet, I kept doing them, but not because I didn't know better, but because opening my heart felt riskier than hurting myself.

Deep down, I believed that no man would ever truly love me. And when you don't believe you're lovable, loving yourself becomes nearly impossible. So, instead of prioritizing my wellbeing, I harmed myself through my decisions. Real healing didn't begin until I allowed God in. I grew up in the church, so I had always known God; faith was never foreign to me. What changed wasn't my belief—it was my distance. During the most turbulent seasons of my life, I believed that my choices had disqualified me from God's presence. I thought that I had to clean up the mess I created before I could invite God back in. Knowing who He was, I felt ashamed that my life didn't reflect what I believed, so instead of turning toward Him, I turned inward. But even then, healing didn't begin when I became stronger, more disciplined, or had more clarity; it began when I surrendered and stopped trying to fix everything on my own. I allowed God into the messiest, ugliest moments of my life and simply asked for help. That surrender changed everything for me.

Before I reached this point, I thought forgiveness meant holding people accountable in my heart. I viewed my anger, resentment, and unforgiveness as justified responses to what they had done to me. But when I got to know God, not just intellectually, but relationally, He showed me who I was through His eyes. He showed me my value, that my body is a temple, and that I only get one life—and that it was worth protecting. It was through Him that I finally saw how much unforgiveness was holding me back, and with this new clarity, I learned to forgive others; not because they deserved it, but because I deserved peace.

Before my relationship with God, I couldn't move forward because I had placed my identity in the hands of too many people, and that is an incredibly unsafe place to live. But my faith taught me that forgiveness required me to shift my focus. Not toward what others had done to me, but toward what I needed to do for myself. Forgiveness does not always mean restarting the relationship. Sometimes, it can be a means of closure. I eventually forgave my first husband, as well as coming to accept that I was also in the wrong during our time together. When we were dating, I had given him an ultimatum. We already had a child, so I told him I wanted to either get married or move on. He chose marriage, but as our relationship unfolded, it was clear that marriage wasn't what he truly wanted. This angered me, but beneath that anger was something deeper: the familiar ache of feeling unchosen. It wasn't fair to him how I ended that marriage, but I didn't see that then. I was operating from wounds I hadn't yet acknowledged.

I didn't understand the process of choosing a partner, a father for your child, and someone to build a life with. I was choosing from desperation, not discernment. He's remarried today, but this level of forgiveness and closure has allowed me to truly love his wife and be happy for him. I even call her "Wifey." She is my oldest daughter's stepmother, and we have a beautiful relationship. I also have a healthy relationship with my ex-husband now—he is still kind and thoughtful, and I pray that he forgives me for how I exited our marriage. I also hope he realizes how much he's helped me on this journey to forgiveness. Years after our divorce, he once said something that stayed with me: "I never understood why you wanted to get married so young." That was the first time I truly heard him. Marriage wasn't what he wanted, but

THE HARDEST PERSON TO FORGIVE OF ALL WAS MYSELF.

he went through with it because it was what I needed at the time to feel safe, chosen, and secure. And understanding that helped me forgive him fully.

You won't always have the "ah-ha" moment with everyone in your life, bringing you to that immediate forgiveness, and sometimes, it'll take less closure and more effort to do so. For example, forgiving my father was harder. At the time, I didn't equate indifference with unforgiveness, so I had convinced myself that cutting people off meant I had moved on. I thought that doing that was enough and that I was fine. But there was an unrest in my spirit, a sense that something was unresolved. I avoided dealing with it, though, because I thought true forgiveness required a conversation or reconciliation, and I wasn't sure I wanted that.

Then, the hardest of all was forgiving my abusive ex because I continued to attempt to reconcile in the forgiveness process, which opened me up for continued torment and turmoil. Every time I called myself "forgiving," I was in so much pain by something he would say or do because I continued to grant him access after another round of "forgiveness," only leading to more pain when the damaging behavior persisted. And because I couldn't break the cycle, I continued to engage in self-harming behavior to cope. So, please understand that forgiveness truly does not have to mean reconciliation, especially when this person does not make an effort to change.

What I eventually learned is this: When someone no longer controls your emotions, when you no longer think of them with resentment, when their presence—or absence—doesn't disrupt your inner calm . . . that is forgiveness. But with that clarity in what forgiveness actually is, came the hardest person to forgive of all: myself. I had spent so much of my life telling myself that I deserved every bad thing that happened, but now that I was accepting a new truth, that I was actually worthy of every good thing life had to offer, I now had to forgive myself for the years of self-abandonment, the choices made from pain, and for the ways I tried to survive when I didn't yet know how to heal. That forgiveness didn't happen overnight, but little by little, it freed me. And now, years later, I am no longer bound to what I did in my past.

So, for anyone who is carrying a similar shame for decisions they're not proud of, I need you to hear this: You are not your worst moment. If you release it, if you ask God for forgiveness and forgive yourself, you can be free, too. When you stop doing the things that hurt you and start choosing what honors you, your life changes. I know my value now. I know my worth. And forgiveness was the first step that made everything else possible. It's what finally calmed the internal anger I kept close. Until I had the strength to really look inward, I had assumed everyone in my life caused all of my anger and resentment, but God showed me I wasn't holding myself accountable. This led me to really look in the mirror, where I discovered that the person who I was most angry with was myself, and that I had only been projecting my pain outward.

Originally, when I started writing this book, I believed I had moved on from all the people who had hurt me, but in reality, I had only postponed the work. But that's okay because healing is not linear. We revisit various chapters of our lives, which I'll introduce to you throughout the pages as we grow. You'll find that we uncover layers when we are ready to hold them. The goal of Face Fear and Live: Twelve Steps to Heal

[...] WHEN THEIR PRESENCE, OR ABSENCE, DOESN'T DISRUPT YOUR INNER CALM

... THAT IS FORGIVENESS.

from What Hurt You is to create self-awareness; if movement follows, great. But at the very least, we should be aware if we are knowingly or unknowingly harboring anger, resentment, and unforgiveness. You can't let go of what you don't know you hold, after all.

Before moving on, I want to invite you to pause for a moment. The words below are here to support you; they are not meant to overwhelm or push you. The scripture shared was something I leaned on when things felt heavy, the affirmations are reminders I needed when my thoughts weren't kind, and the reflection questions are simply an opportunity to notice what's coming to the surface for you. Engage how you feel most comfortable. Take what resonates, skip what doesn't, and move at a pace that feels manageable.

SCRIPTURE FOR REFLECTION

"Get rid of all bitterness, rage and anger . . . forgiving each other, just as in Christ God forgave you." Ephesians 4:31–32

AFFIRMATION

I release what no longer serves me. I forgive to free myself. I am not bound to my past. I choose healing, peace, and wholeness.

GENTLE REFLECTION

What am I holding onto that is costing me peace?
What would freedom look like if I released it?

2

ACCEPT

The Life That Is

|

For a long time, I didn't realize I was resisting acceptance, and this proved to be the most challenging lesson for me. When it came to being a single mother of three, I struggled with accepting that reality felt like a personal failure. My mom was a single mom. Her mom was a single mom. I had so badly wanted to break the cycle. So, when my relationship dreams were shattered, I felt like history was repeating itself, and instead of accepting my reality, I resisted it. I held tightly to relationships that had already expired. I tried to insert men into my life, not because they were healthy or aligned with what I did want for myself, but because I was desperate to create an intact family. I believed that if I could just make it look whole, then it would feel whole. But it was in not accepting my reality that I became stuck in unforgiveness—toward others and myself. This was mentally, physically, emotionally, and spiritually exhausting. I eventually grew tired of trying to fix my life instead of accepting it. Every time I attempted to "fix" my reality by inserting a man, I felt like I was abandoning myself and my children. It was as if I was sending the message that we weren't good enough on our own, and that belief quietly eroded my sense of worth.

My oldest child has cerebral palsy and an intellectual disability. She required immense care, attention, advocacy, and patience. I worried constantly about her, about whether she would connect, belong, or feel seen. My youngest was born twelve weeks premature and struggled with asthma and fragile lungs. My middle child, born ten weeks premature, was quiet, withdrawn, and often isolated. Caring for each of them individually was demanding. Caring for all of them together was overwhelming, especially because I had limited support. I worked full-time, and still, I was financially stretched. This is when I made the decision to go back to school because I knew I needed to increase my income to better support my children. But internally, I was still fighting my reality instead of accepting it. And that resistance made everything heavier. In resisting acceptance, I missed vital moments in my children's lives. I was physically present but emotionally distracted, focusing only on trying to change my circumstances and fix what felt wrong. I struggled to be fully in the moments that mattered most right in front of me.

Acceptance didn't happen all at once. It came gradually, alongside forgiveness. When I first began accepting that I was a single mother of three, something shifted. My children no longer felt like a burden. Raising them didn't feel "hard" in the same way. I started to see them not as obstacles to the life I wanted, but as the life I was living, and it was beautiful. Each of my children brought something unique to our family. My youngest child was the jokester, always making people laugh. My middle child was the logical one, thoughtful, practical, always considering the bigger picture. She was the one reminding her siblings to eat leftovers so that Mom didn't have to spend money eating out. My oldest child was pure joy, a party in a box. She woke up singing. She went to bed singing. Nothing dimmed her desire to enjoy life.

Together, we became me and my three. And we began to thrive. We went to church, attended activities together, and hosted gatherings in our home. They brought joy into my life, and I made them my priority. I understood deeply that my primary role was mother—and everything else was secondary. No one came before my children (except God), which is when I decided I needed to put dating aside for now. This level of sacrifice allowed them to watch my healing journey. They watched my faith grow as I chose acceptance instead of bitterness. And they grew into amazing humans who loved the Lord and loved their mother fiercely.

I want to be honest, acceptance didn't erase the pain of everything I had gone through, but acceptance allowed me to stop fighting what was and start stewarding what is. Acceptance doesn't mean you approve of what happened to you. It means you stop letting it control you. What happened to you happened to you, but it is not you. And once you accept that truth, you can finally move on.

SCRIPTURE FOR REFLECTION

"Forget the former things; do not dwell on the past."

—Isaiah 43:18

AFFIRMATIONS

I accept my life as it is today.

What happened to me does not define me.

I release shame, blame, and guilt.

I am allowed to move forward with grace.

GENTLE REFLECTION

What part of my reality am I resisting? And how might acceptance bring peace instead of pain?

3

COURAGE

Feel Fear and Do It Anyway

Fear consumed large portions of my life, especially after abuse. It didn't always look dramatic, though. Sometimes, it looked like hesitation. Sometimes, it looked like overthinking. And sometimes, it looked like silence. But fear had a voice, and for a long time, I listened to it more than I listened to myself. Fear told me:

"Don't trust your instincts."

"If you try, you will fail."

"Staying small is safer than taking risks."

After experiencing betrayal, abandonment, and abuse, fear felt logical. It felt protective. However, what I didn't realize at the time was that fear was no longer keeping me safe—it was keeping me stuck.

When courage finally arrived, it didn't arrive as confidence, as I once thought it would. Instead, it arrived as confrontation. I had to confront the false evidence appearing real, the lies that told me I wasn't capable, wasn't strong enough, and wasn't worthy of more. I had to confront the version of myself that learned to survive by shrinking. I found that courage also required honesty. I had to look at myself and admit where I was wounded and where trauma had shaped my reactions, my patterns, my behaviors, my relationships, and my self-esteem. Finally, courage required me to acknowledge my greatness: I was resilient, persistent, and still showed up for my children every day. For a long time, I focused only on what was wrong with me. Courage invited balance, inviting me to see myself fully, wounded and worthy.

But before I could fully confront fear, I had to take inventory and identify areas of my life that needed attention; areas where my self-esteem had been damaged, where I doubted my ability to succeed, and where fear dictated my choices. I had to name specific fears instead of letting them remain vague and overpowering.

Fear of being alone.
Fear of failure.
Fear of rejection.
Fear of repeating the past.

FEAR
THRIVES IN
ISOLATION

IT IS
COURAGE
THAT
GROWS IN
CONNECTION.

Courage doesn't eliminate fear, but it makes it lose some of its power, allowing you to move forward. There were moments when courage meant taking action without certainty: applying for job opportunities I wasn't sure I deserved, speaking up when my voice shook, setting boundaries with family and friends, even when guilt followed, or choosing growth when comfort called me back. But I had to learn how to embrace the vulnerability of putting myself out there. I had to be transparent with myself about what I wanted. And at the same time, I had to be honest with myself and those around me about what I was struggling with. In order to keep having the confidence to move forward, I had to allow others to support me, which was something that felt foreign after years of believing I had to do everything alone. But fear thrives in isolation. It is courage that grows in connection. Every courageous step I took, no matter how small, strengthened me. Each step reinforced the truth that I was capable of more than fear had ever allowed me to believe.

The Bible tells us that God has not given us a spirit of fear, and I believe that with my whole heart. That does not mean, however, that fear will never be present. Genuine fear does exist in this world. It shows up in our bodies, our thoughts, and our memories—especially after trauma. What it does mean, though, is that fear does not get the final word. It means that fear is a response, not a reflection of our faith.

For a long time, I believed that feeling afraid meant I was failing spiritually. That was another belief that kept me stuck. What I eventually learned is that courage doesn't require the absence of fear; it requires movement despite it. The understanding that fear can be present, but it does not get to lead, changed everything for me. I even got a tattoo that says "Do it scared," a reminder that even when fear is present, I am still allowed to move forward. I don't need to wait until I feel fearless to take the next step. I just need to be willing.

> Courage is not loud.
> Courage is not reckless.
> Courage is choosing action while fear watches
>   from the sidelines.
> Courage is choosing yourself again and again,
>   even when fear is present.

And once you confront fear, you begin to conquer it. Every courageous act, no matter the cost, leaves you with proof that you did it, that you survived, and that you are still standing. And that proof becomes strength for the next step.

"COURAGE DOESN'T REQUIRE THE ABSENCE OF FEAR; IT REQUIRES MOVEMENT DESPITE IT."

SCRIPTURE FOR REFLECTION

"For God has not given us a spirit of fear, but of power, love, and a sound mind." —2 Timothy 1:7

AFFIRMATIONS

I am courageous even when I feel afraid.

I confront fear with truth and action.

I trust myself to move forward.

Fear does not control my future.

GENTLE REFLECTION

What fear has been holding me back? And what courageous step can I take, even if it's small?

I HAD TO
IDENTIFY
BELIEFS THAT
WERE ROOTED
IN FEAR RATHER
THAN REALITY;
BELIEFS THAT
TOLD ME
I WOULD
ALWAYS
STRUGGLE [...]

4

ELIMINATE

The Space You Create to Heal

There comes a point in healing when awareness alone is no longer enough. You can forgive. You can accept. You can even act courageously. But if you continue allowing the same negative influences, thought patterns, and environments into your life, healing can burn you out. I had to learn this the hard way. I was trying to heal in spaces that were still harming me. I was attempting to grow while still surrounded by people, patterns, and habits that kept pulling me backward. Simply put, I was asking my heart to recover while my mind was constantly being fed damaging thoughts.

In a world with endless avenues for negativity, it is vital to be intentional about what you allow into your mind. It is about recognizing what no longer serves you, grows you, or makes you better—and then choosing not to carry it forward. For me, one of the first things I had to eliminate was negative self-talk, but it wasn't as straightforward as it may sound. It was subtle, quiet, and familiar, and I didn't always hear it clearly at first. But when I really started to pay attention, I realized that it sounded like doubt, second-guessing, minimizing my progress, and telling myself I should be further along by now. Once I became aware of it, I saw how powerful it had been. My inner dialogue was shaping my confidence, my decisions, and my sense of worth. So, when I set out to eliminate negative self-talk, it meant intentionally replacing it with truth. It also meant addressing my negative mindset toward certain areas of my life. I had to identify beliefs that were rooted in fear rather than reality; beliefs that told me I would always struggle, that things wouldn't work out, and that I shouldn't expect more. Those mindsets didn't come from truth—they came from trauma.

And then came one of the hardest eliminations of all: people. Not everyone who has access to you deserves proximity. Some people drain you, discourage you, or subtly undermine your growth (not always with ill intent, but consistently). I had to become honest about how certain interactions made me feel. If I left conversations defeated, anxious, or diminished, I had to ask myself, "Why am I allowing that energy into my life?" But elimination and limiting access are not about becoming cold or cutting people off impulsively. Elimination requires boundaries, and although it may feel like it at first,

AND THEN
CAME ONE OF
THE HARDEST
ELIMINATIONS
OF ALL:
PEOPLE.

boundaries are not punishment. They are protection. They are the guardrails that keep you moving forward without constantly falling back into old patterns.

I didn't learn boundaries in theory; I learned them in actual moments, when my choices directly affected my peace and my children. My children knew I was dating someone. They met him. They liked him. We spent time together every other weekend and one day during the week. However, when he expressed it wasn't enough time for us to grow a relationship, I made a decision that defined this chapter of my life: My primary role is mother, not girlfriend. This choice ended the relationship. But even though I was heartbroken when he ended things, I did not regret choosing my children.

When I first started setting boundaries, I felt uncomfortable. Limiting access felt selfish, and saying no felt wrong. Eventually, I accepted that it is something that requires practice, especially as life evolves and new situations arise. Even now, I still have to remind myself why boundaries matter—and every time I choose to honor my needs, even when it feels uncomfortable, I know I am choosing my healing. Protecting my peace is not optional.

Elimination also meant letting go of comfort. In phases of dysfunction, things still felt familiar and predictable, offering an unexpected sense of safety. But that kind of comfort does not always equal health. Growth often requires stepping away from what feels known and stepping toward what feels unfamiliar, and eliminating the extra created space to do that.

Space for peace.
Space for clarity.
Space for joy.
Space for healing to finally breathe.

And these are the new things that are already waiting for you.

SCRIPTURE FOR REFLECTION

"Do not conform to the pattern of this world, but be transformed
by the renewing of your mind." —Romans 12:2

AFFIRMATIONS

I release what no longer serves me.

I protect my peace with healthy boundaries.

I choose environments that support my growth.

I am allowed to let go.

GENTLE REFLECTION

What thoughts, patterns, behaviors, habits, or relationships
am I being invited to release so I can continue healing?

02

RECLAIMING YOUR LIFE

5

FREE

You Deserve to Breathe and Dream

When fear, unforgiveness, anger, and bitterness have a hold on you, you are not free, even if your life looks functional on the outside. In Chapter 1, I mentioned that I didn't realize how much unforgiveness was shaping my life and how bound I was because of this. I thought freedom meant independence, not needing anyone, and surviving on my own terms, but in truth, freedom meant releasing fear and limiting beliefs and finally choosing myself without guilt. This didn't arrive until I let go.

Let go of what I could not change.
Let go of what I was never meant to carry.
Let go of the belief that my past had the
  authority to dictate my future.

When I forgave, something loosened. When I accepted, something softened. When I acted courageously and eliminated what no longer served me, something opened. And suddenly, I could breathe.

Freedom invited curiosity back into my life. I began exploring what I actually liked—not what I thought I should like. I noticed what brought me joy and what drained me. I paid attention to what energized me and what felt heavy. There were things I enjoyed that surprised me, and there were things I tolerated for far too long that I finally admitted I didn't want anymore. Freedom gave me permission to say, "This no longer fits me." And that was okay. For the first time in a long time, I allowed myself to freely dream about my future.

Dreaming didn't begin with specific goals or neatly defined outcomes. It began with the acceptance that I was no longer bound by the need to be accepted, the weight of unforgiveness, or the fear of getting it wrong. For so long, survival had required me to stay small, predictable, and restrained. Dreaming didn't feel like it was available to me then. Now, it did. I felt a sense of ownership over my life for the first time. It was a quiet but powerful understanding that I could choose how I wanted to live, who I wanted to become, and what I wanted to move toward. This was my opportunity to identify what mattered to me, what energized me, and how I wanted to navigate my life going forward, without guilt, fear, or anything holding me back.

At first, limiting beliefs tried to re-enter the conversation when I started to dream. Fear whispered reminders of the past. But freedom taught me that dreams don't need guarantees to be valid. They just need permission. Permission from myself to trust my instincts, to want more, and to believe I could have more and build a life that felt safe, aligned, and whole. So, to remind me of what I was working toward, especially during moments of discouragement, I began setting goals to honor the version of myself I was becoming. Some goals felt bold. Some felt intimidating. But all of them were rooted in possibility rather than fear. Freedom also taught me structure. Dreams without direction stay wishes, so I learned to break goals down into small, attainable steps that built momentum and confidence. I didn't need to see the entire path; I just needed to take the next right step. And with each step, freedom expanded.

For me, that looked like returning to school because increasing my education increased my options. Through grants and student loans, it allowed me to grow into an expert in my field while also providing additional income to help stabilize my life as a newly single mother of three. It looked like starting a retirement account, an act that felt minor at the time but quietly laid the groundwork for future stability. Years later, that decision made it possible for me to pull together a down payment on the first home I would purchase on my own for my children and me. That property came with a rental unit, so I even became a landlord with instant passive income. It also looked like starting my nonprofit, which didn't begin with a grand vision or a polished plan. It began with a conversation. I met someone who had done it before, asked questions, listened, learned, and took one step at a time. None of these steps felt dramatic, but together, they changed my life. Each one reinforced the same truth: I didn't need to have all the answers to move forward. I needed to trust in myself, in my decisions, and in my ability to build a life piece by piece.

Freedom gave me something I had longed for but hadn't experienced since my younger years: stability, love, joy, comfort, and support. Even so, being free doesn't mean life becomes easy, but it does mean you stop living restrained by what hurts you. It means you reclaim your right to imagine, create, and pursue a life that feels aligned. Freedom is the space where healing turns into hope.

SCRIPTURE FOR REFLECTION

"It is for freedom that Christ has set us free. Stand firm, then, and do not let yourselves be burdened again by a yoke of slavery." —Galatians 5:1

AFFIRMATIONS

I am free to dream without limitations.
I release what once bound me.
I choose possibility over fear.
My future is open and mine to create.

GENTLE REFLECTION

If nothing were holding me back, what would I allow myself to dream about? And what is one small step I could take toward it?

YOU DO NOT
BECOME
COURAGEOUS
ONCE AND
THEN NEVER
FEEL FEAR
AGAIN.

6

EMPOWER

*Taking Your Power Back,
One Choice at a Time*

Overcoming challenges is empowering. Not because the challenges disappear, but because you change in the process of moving through them.

Empowerment is an intentional decision to take your power back. The process that follows supports it. Step by step, naturally and strategically, your choices begin to align with who you are becoming. Empowerment comes from persistence and from choosing yourself again and again, even when parts of you are still learning and still letting go.

I want to pause here to remind you of something important: Healing is not linear. You do not master forgiveness and then never revisit it. You do not fully accept your life and then suddenly stop wrestling with disappointment. You do not become courageous once and then never feel fear again. These steps are not boxes you check off; they are tools you return to. You will weave in and out of these chapters throughout your entire life. You may still be holding some unforgiveness, but you can still move into acceptance. You may be struggling to fully accept parts of your life, but you can still move courageously. When something you thought you had already worked through resurfaces, meet yourself with grace and compassion. It's part of the human experience. Healing requires awareness, so look at it as a new opportunity to peel back another layer of healing from your past.

Empowerment comes when you understand what you're experiencing and why, and when you recognize that something unresolved is showing up again, not to shame you, but to invite deeper healing. Another part of empowering yourself is gratitude, not just for what you have, but for what you've overcome. For me, empowerment began when I stopped judging myself for where I was and started honoring the progress I had made. Your past is not something to be embarrassed about. It is evidence of your resilience. So, embrace it and let it strengthen you instead of haunt you.

Empowerment is a means of taking your power back. It's choosing responsibility without self-blame. It's recognizing where you still have influence and agency. It's brainstorming options instead of staying stuck in limitations. It's asking, "What can I do with what I have, right now?" Everyone makes

YOUR PAST
IS NOT
SOMETHING
TO BE
EMBARRASSED
ABOUT. IT IS
EVIDENCE
OF YOUR
RESILIENCE.

mistakes. Owning them strengthens your story. The things you've survived, learned, and grown through are part of what gives your story meaning and power. When you release shame, you step more fully into who you are.

Empowerment often begins with small, intentional choices:

How you care for your body
How you speak to yourself
How you show up each day
How you keep promises to yourself

Your confidence grows when you follow through, and your confidence erodes when you repeatedly abandon yourself. For example, when you tell yourself you're going to rest, nourish yourself, or move your body, and then you follow through, your confidence strengthens. But when you repeatedly say, "I'll take care of myself later," and later never comes, your body learns that your needs are negotiable. Is that the message you want to send yourself? If you commit to replacing self-criticism with compassion and then catch yourself mid-spiral and choose a kinder thought, confidence grows. You've proven to yourself that you can interrupt old patterns. But when you promise to be gentler with yourself and continue using language that diminishes you, your confidence takes a hit because the promise was broken.

Showing up for yourself means doing something: attending the appointment, submitting the application, making the call, even when it's uncomfortable. Each follow-through becomes evidence that you are capable. When you avoid, delay, or disappear from your own commitments, doubt steps in and begins to question your reliability to protect you from disappointment. Confidence is about self-trust, and self-trust is built through kept promises.

This season of empowerment is a posture. You will continue to return here, and each time, life will ask more of you. But every time, healing and courage will also deepen. You are practicing self-trust, and self-trust is the foundation of empowerment. You are becoming on purpose.

SCRIPTURE FOR REFLECTION

"I can do all things through Christ who strengthens me."
—Philippians 4:13

AFFIRMATIONS

I am empowered, even while I am healing.

I give myself grace as I grow.

I reclaim my power with intention and compassion.

I trust myself to return to what I need.

GENTLE REFLECTION

Where in my life am I being invited to reclaim my power,
without judging where I still need healing?

7

AFFIRM

Letting Belief Take Root

When I was struggling to believe I was worthy of good things happening to me, there was still a quiet voice that questioned whether I deserved more. I doubted my abilities, I questioned my readiness, and sometimes, without realizing it, I sabotaged myself with feelings of unworthiness. When I was offered opportunities to lead trainings, speak on panels, and share my expertise, I hesitated. I questioned whether I was ready, whether I was qualified enough, whether my voice belonged there. Sometimes, I declined the opportunity altogether. Other times, I asked for additional support that reduced my compensation or my visibility, despite being the one doing the majority of the work. More than once, I watched someone else accept an opportunity I had turned down and realized, as I listened, I could have done that. Not because I suddenly became capable in hindsight, but because I had been capable all along. The difference wasn't skill or intelligence; it was belief. I didn't trust my own readiness. I didn't believe I was enough. And in those moments, unworthiness didn't just affect how I felt about myself; it limited what I allowed myself to receive.

Affirmation became the bridge between who I was and who I was becoming. During this stage of the journey, affirmations became my roadmap. To affirm is not simply to say positive words—it is to agree with the truth. It is to speak life over yourself in moments when fear, doubt, or old narratives try to take the lead. Affirmation is how belief takes root. That's why I have added affirmations at the end of each chapter. I saw firsthand how life-changing they are. They reminded me of what was possible when I aligned my thoughts with intention and faith. They helped me move from healing into attainment. This led me to revisit the goals I had identified during my season of freedom. Some goals stayed the same, others evolved, and both were okay.

I learned to identify "I am" statements that supported the future I was working toward:

I am capable.
I am intelligent.
I am disciplined.
I am worthy of success.

There are many forms of affirmations: I will, I can, I choose, I deserve. Each has value, but I intentionally centered my practice around "I am" statements because they speak directly to identity. After trauma, self-doubt doesn't usually attack our goals first; it attacks who we believe we are. "I am" statements helped me reclaim authorship over my identity at a time when I had outsourced my worth to fear, trauma, survival, and other people's approval. "I am" statements brought the work back to the one place I still had control: myself. When I said, "I am intelligent. I am disciplined. I am worthy of success and a healthy love," I wasn't trying to convince myself of something new. I was naming what had already been true but buried under years of doubt. These affirmations weren't aspirational–they were restorative and helped me return to myself.

"THESE AFFIRMATIONS
WEREN'T ASPIRATIONAL
THEY WERE RESTORATIVE
AND HELPED ME
RETURN TO MYSELF"

But affirmation is not about standing in front of the mirror, repeating words you don't believe. It's about speaking truth until belief catches up. It's about letting those words move from your mouth to your heart to your actions. And when affirmation becomes embodied, everything shifts.

I don't believe healing requires a rigid affirmation ritual. For me, affirmations become most powerful when they're responsive rather than routine. When doubt began to creep in, when imposter syndrome whispered that I wasn't ready or capable, I paused long enough to ask, "Is this actually true?" And then, I answered that doubt with the truth. Sometimes, that truth was spoken out loud. Sometimes, it was said quietly in my mind. Sometimes, it was reflected to me from affirmations posted in my workspace. And other times, it came naturally while standing in front of the mirror as I got ready for the day, feeling grounded in my body, energized by movement, sunlight, or momentum. In those moments, I made sure to name what I was feeling and reinforced it with intention. Affirmations worked for me because I used them honestly. They became a way to interrupt old narratives and choose a truer one in real time, and over time, those interruptions became habits, and those habits reshaped beliefs.

As my healing deepened, I chose to formalize the work I had already been doing intuitively. I completed a six-month coaching certification program and became a certified coach with a focus on self-awareness, relationship trauma, and emotional healing. I was learning how to help others examine patterns, build emotional literacy, and prepare for healthier relationships, while still actively practicing

TO AFFIRM
IS NOT
SIMPLY TO
SAY POSITIVE
WORDS
IT IS TO AGREE
WITH THE
TRUTH.

those same principles in my own life. And it was that space, holding both growth and responsibility, that doubt quietly resurfaced. When beginning to say affirmations, it may feel uncomfortable at first. Or, if you're like me, affirming yourself may even feel dishonest. I struggled deeply with imposter syndrome, especially when I stepped into calling myself a coach. I would think, who am I to coach anyone? I had two failed relationships. I had made choices that didn't honor myself. I had lived through patterns I was still healing from. I questioned whether I had the right to lead others in relationships when my own history felt messy. I believed that credibility came from what appeared to look successful, and that belief kept me stuck.

So, when I decided to fully embrace affirmations, I reminded myself that I wasn't pretending I hadn't struggled. Telling myself these "I am" statements was about owning who I had become because of the struggles. It was about allowing my lived experience to become wisdom instead of shame. This helped me fully understand that healing does not disqualify you—it qualifies you. Wisdom does not come from never falling; it comes from getting back up with awareness and intention. If you continue to struggle with affirmations, identify a support person who can walk with you in this. With the support of my now husband, I began to believe something new about myself. I didn't just survive hard things. I was capable of creating meaningful work. I was allowed to pursue what mattered to me. And I didn't have to do it alone. That belief changed everything, so much so that I made the decision to leave my corporate job, a role that had provided security, stability, and medical benefits, but no longer aligned with the life I was building. I became my daughter's primary caregiver and began pursuing my passion in a real, tangible way. This was the moment my nonprofit stopped being a side hustle and started becoming a calling in action. In 2022, we officially opened the doors of Healed Women Heal with the help of a few small grants. Every time I had feelings of incompetence, my husband said, "You got this, babe," and I would reply, "I am a business owner. I have a successful nonprofit. I am learning every day." And what followed was something I could not have built alone.

I became deeply rooted in my community. Partnerships were established. Collaborations Built. Affirming relationships formed that allowed the organization (and me) to grow with integrity and credibility. Healed Women Heal began to be recognized as a reputable nonprofit supporting and advocating for those impacted by domestic violence because I was surrounded by people who believed in the mission. At the leadership level, affirming relationships began to take shape. We partnered with legislative officials, city leaders, business owners, and community organizations.

So, as you start your affirmations, don't be afraid to take small steps. The momentum will pick up naturally as you go. You can begin by asking yourself:

Who affirms who I am becoming?
Where do I feel supported, not drained?
What environments allow me to grow without shrinking?
What would expand if I stopped doing life alone?

Affirmations aren't meant to just feel good—they are meant to help you build lives, legacies, and communities. And you don't need everyone to affirm you to do this. You just need the right people. Today, when that voice tries to resurface, asking, "Who do you think you are? Do you really think you're qualified?" I ask myself two questions: Why not me? Why not the woman who has lived it, learned from it, healed through it, and can now speak truth with compassion and clarity? Because my healing was intentional. And that is what makes affirmations real for me. So, to that voice asking who do I think I am and do I really think I'm qualified, the answer is, I am a coach. I am a self-awareness and relationship coach. And yes! Yes, I am qualified.

SCRIPTURE FOR REFLECTION

"As a man thinks in his heart, so is he." —Proverbs 23:7

AFFIRMATIONS

I am worthy of the life I am building.

I believe in my ability to succeed.

I align my thoughts, words, and actions with truth.

I affirm who I am becoming.

GENTLE REFLECTION

What belief about myself needs to shift so my actions can align with the life I desire?

8

RENEW

You Get to Choose

Renewal is an act of intentional realignment. It is the decision to stop living on autopilot and begin living with awareness and choice. It is choosing to update the way you see yourself, the way you think about your life, and the way you respond to opportunity. As I mentioned in previous chapters, limiting beliefs kept me from pursuing things I truly wanted, even attaching themselves to my identity. Those beliefs were subtle but persistent. They questioned my readiness, my worth, and whether I had earned the right to desire more. Some of these beliefs sounded like:

- That's not who I am.
- People like me don't do things like that.
- I'm too late.
- I'm not qualified.
- I missed my chance.

Renewal required me to intentionally challenge those thoughts. This meant I had to re-identify myself, and just like I did before I could confront fear, I had to take inventory of my life. I started by asking honest questions about where I was thriving and where I was merely surviving. I began looking at different areas of my life: career, finances, health, fitness, relationships, joy, travel, rest, and notice where my beliefs were either supporting or sabotaging my growth.

Renewal took shape every time I chose alignment over familiarity. I had to get real with myself and identify what I wanted to pursue, and not just do what was easy. It was built through small, intentional decisions to do things differently than I had before, especially when continuing the same patterns was no longer serving me.

Throughout the process, my goal was never to become someone else; it was to return to myself, the version of me that existed before disappointment started making decisions on my behalf. Who is that person? But renewal is awareness in motion, so once I identified areas that were suffering, I knew not to shame myself. Instead, I became curious. I asked, "What belief is operating here? And is it true?" Often, the answer to the second one was no.

This stage of the journey invited intentional reinvestment. Sometimes, that meant education. Sometimes, it meant rest.

Sometimes, it meant saying no. And sometimes, it meant saying yes to things that felt exciting and uncomfortable at the same time. I once saw a post on Instagram that stopped me in my tracks: Be willing to risk it all and confident enough to get it all back. That idea felt both scary and exhilarating. And then, I realized, the feeling wasn't fear. It was expansion. Renewal often feels like that. Not reckless. Not impulsive. But expansive, like stepping into alignment with who you've always known you could become.

Renewal required me to make intentional decisions to better my life with clarity. It was the moment I stopped minimizing my education, my experience, and the survival that had shaped me. I stopped treating what I had lived through as something separate from my professional capacity and began honoring it as preparation. I had walked people through dark, private places they felt unable to share with anyone else because I understood those spaces firsthand. That clarity gave birth to Tracy's Healing Room. It wasn't a reinvention; it was alignment. I wasn't becoming this work, I had already become it.

At the same time, renewal demanded structure. My husband and I faced the weight of accumulated debt (from life, marriage, and responsibility), and chose to address it directly. With my father's guidance and support, we committed to eliminating it fully. We worked relentlessly, sacrificed comfort, and redirected every available resource toward stability. In two years, we eliminated $110,000 in debt, built savings, and created margin. That work didn't just change our finances; it strengthened our marriage, our confidence, and our capacity to make grounded decisions. It also made our next step possible.

With stability restored and clarity about who I was called to serve, we relocated our business to a city more aligned with our vision and the outcomes we were building toward. Renewal had positioned us emotionally, financially, and strategically to choose alignment over fear.

Renewing yourself means believing that growth is still available to you. That opportunity is still accessible. That nothing is wasted—not the pain, not the waiting, not the detours. You are intentionally putting yourself together, piece by piece, with purpose and care. And that kind of renewal changes everything.

SCRIPTURE FOR REFLECTION

"See, I am doing a new thing! Now it springs up;
do you not perceive it?" —Isaiah 43:19

AFFIRMATION

I am worthy of reinvestment.
I release limiting beliefs that no longer serve me.
I renew my mind with truth and intention.
I am becoming my best self—continually.

GENTLE REFLECTION

Where in my life am I being invited to renew my way of thinking,
choosing, or responding? And what is one small, intentional
shift I could make to support the person I am becoming?

03

LIVING FROM
WHOLENESS

BUT
ABOVE
ALL,
LOVE
SHOULD
NOT
HURT.

9

LOVE

The Greatest Gift

For a long time, I believed love was something you gave away, something you earned, negotiated, or sacrificed yourself for. I didn't yet understand that loving others cannot be separated from loving yourself and that love offered from a place of hurt, resentment, or self-abandonment is not sustainable. Love received from that same place is difficult to trust.

Unhealed love often carries:

Fear of abandonment
Need for validation

Desire for control
Urgency to be chosen

But above all, love should not hurt.

That truth took time to settle in my spirit. When your heart is filled with unforgiveness, anger, fear, and unresolved trauma, there simply isn't enough room for love to fully occupy the space. Hurt crowds it out. Survival instincts take over. Self-protection becomes the priority. But when you begin to heal and forgive, accept, act courageously, eliminate what no longer serves you, choose freedom, empower yourself, affirm truth, and renew your mind, something shifts. There is room for love to enter.

This chapter is about learning to love from a healed place, starting with yourself. Many people think loving yourself is done in vanity, but the truth is, it is caring for what God has entrusted to you: your body, your mind, your heart, and your life. Loving yourself means practicing self-care regularly as a responsibility. It means honoring your body with gratitude instead of criticism. It means being intentional about how you look and feel—not for approval, but for alignment. It means inviting gentleness inward.

As I learned to love myself, I also became more intentional about who I surrounded myself with. I knew that love grows best in environments where encouragement is present, where safety exists, and where growth is supported rather than threatened. But I also knew that those same things needed to come from me. I had to recognize my strengths, abilities, and gifts, and because love is generous, flowing outward naturally when it is rooted in wholeness rather than depletion, I could then give my strengths away freely.

LOVE IS THE GREATEST GIFT, [...] BECAUSE IT EMERGES WHEN PAIN HAS BEEN TENDED TO.

"ONCE LOVE BECOMES YOUR POSTURE, EVERYTHING ELSE BEGINS TO ALIGN AROUND IT."

Love is the greatest gift, not because it ignores pain, but because it emerges when pain has been tended to. And once love becomes your posture, everything else begins to align around it. It was in this season that I learned the power of giving and receiving compliments without deflection, without discomfort, and without disbelief. I learned to believe that I was worthy of love, deserving of kindness, and allowed to receive goodness without suspicion. Random acts of kindness became expressions of overflow rather than obligation. Compassion became easier when my heart was no longer weighed down by pain or the feeling of having no options. Joy became more accessible, peace more familiar. When love takes root, it changes how you move through the world.

You soften.
You smile more easily.

Your face reflects peace instead of tension. You find that you can hold space for others because your heart is no longer crowded with unresolved hurt.

SCRIPTURE FOR REFLECTION

"Above all, love each other deeply, because love covers over a multitude of sins." —1 Peter 4:8

AFFIRMATIONS

I love myself with compassion and care.

I am worthy of love that is healthy and kind.

My heart is open to give and receive love freely.

Love flows through me from a place of wholeness.

GENTLE REFLECTION

How can I show love to myself today in a way that honors my healing and my worth?

10

INSPIRE

When Healing Becomes a Calling

When someone overcomes great obstacles in life and gets back on track, they are admired. But when someone overcomes great obstacles and chooses to pave a new path, they become an inspiration. As such, there is a responsibility attached to healing—not a burden, but a calling. This stage of the journey is not about putting yourself on display or pretending you have it all figured out. It is about recognizing the quiet power of your testimony. The things that once threatened to break you now carry the ability to give someone else hope.

That matters.

There was a time when I couldn't lift my head to make eye contact or offer a smile without effort. I felt hopeless, defeated, and unsure if life would ever feel light again. And now, here I am, with my head held high, shoulders back, and my peace present. The people in my life noticed the shift long before I realized it myself. They didn't need to know every detail of my story to see the evidence of healing. They simply saw someone who had endured and emerged differently. "How?" they asked. Most often, this question came from clients who were still early in their healing. They would say things like, "I look up to you," or "I just want to get to where you are," or "How did you get to this place?" Those comments always made me uncomfortable because I never wanted to be seen as someone who had arrived. I knew how hard the work was, and I was still doing it. But this is exactly where inspiration lives.

The obstacles you've overcome have given you a kind of wisdom that cannot be taught in a classroom. You now carry perspective, compassion, and insight that others desperately need. That thing meant to break you is now the very thing that qualifies you to lead with empathy and authenticity. You have influence, whether you recognize it yet or not.

Inspiring others doesn't mean reliving your pain; it means allowing your healing to speak, and you don't need a platform to do this. All you need is presence. It'll show up in conversations, in consistency, in the way you treat others, and in the courage to be honest about where you've been and where you're going. So, as you live in a way that offers hope without pressure, encouragement without comparison, and truth without judgment, become mindful of the people watching you, the ones silently drawing strength from your journey.

You don't inspire by telling people what to do.
You inspire by showing what's possible.
Inspiration invites you to ask:

What parts of my story could free someone else?
Where am I hiding pain that could actually
    become purpose?
What would shift if I shared truth instead
    of perfection?
Who might be waiting for me to speak?

And as you continue forward, remember this: Inspiration is not something you turn on and off. It is a posture, growing as you grow.

I have always associated growth and healing with inspiration, but I once experienced something that made me realize this perspective is not always the case. It had me pause and really reflect on what inspiration looks like, and why it can feel so threatening. I had facilitated an empowerment class with a group of powerful, accomplished women. At the end, we took a group photo together, one that captured a moment that felt celebratory, honest, and proud. I shared that photo in my newsletter as a reflection of courage, growth, and community, but almost immediately, one woman called me and asked that the photo be taken down. She explained that she could not risk people knowing she had participated in something like this. In her high-level leadership role, she felt that being associated with an empowerment or healing space would create what she called a chink in her armor. She feared it would make her appear weak.

INSPIRATION
IS NOT
SOMETHING
YOU TURN
ON & OFF.
IT IS
A POSTURE,
GROWING
AS YOU
GROW.

"INSPIRATION IS NOT ABOUT EXPOSURE FOR EXPOSURE'S SAKE. IT'S ABOUT DISCERNMENT."

I honored her request and removed the photo, but the moment stayed with me. What she perceived as weakness, I saw as strength. What she feared would diminish her credibility, I believed would deepen it. It then became clear to me just how extremely conditioned many of us are to equate vulnerability with failure, especially in positions of influence. Inspiration can feel dangerous when we've learned to survive by appearing unshakable, but healing is not weakness, seeking growth is not incompetence, and acknowledging that we are human does not take away from our leadership—it enhances it.

This experience reminded me that inspiration is not about exposure for exposure's sake. It's about discernment. It's about choosing when, how, and with whom we share our healing journey with—not about hiding altogether. You don't owe the world your wounds, but you also don't need to armor yourself against growth. True inspiration doesn't demand vulnerability, but it does invite it. And when someone chooses to step into that invitation, even quietly, it creates ripples far beyond what they can see. So, I dare you to be an inspiration, not by striving, but by standing fully in who you've become.

SCRIPTURE FOR REFLECTION
"Let your light shine before others, that they may see your good deeds and glorify your Father in heaven." —Matthew 5:16

AFFIRMATIONS
My life offers hope to others.
I lead with authenticity and compassion.
My story has purpose and impact.
I inspire by living in truth.

GENTLE REFLECTION
Who might be encouraged simply by seeing me live, healed and whole? And how can I show up with intention?

THE
INVESTMENT
YOU PLACE
INTO
YOURSELF
INCREASES
YOUR VALUE.

11

VALUE

Your Worth Was Never the Question

There is no finish line to personal growth, no moment where you "arrive" and stop developing. But the more you invest in yourself, the closer you get. And the harder you work with intention, the better you become.

You are valuable simply because you exist.

I had always underestimated my value because I tied it to outcomes instead of effort. I measured worth by perfection instead of persistence. I didn't yet understand that value is built serenely, through discipline, learning, humility, and consistency.

Every course taken.
Every book read.
Every pattern examined.
Every adjustment made.
All of it mattered.

The investment you place into yourself (emotionally, spiritually, intellectually) increases your value. Not in a performative way, but in a practical one. You become more skilled. More insightful. More equipped to serve. And service is where value becomes visible.

It's important to recognize self-investment as a responsibility, not as an indulgence. Developing and fine-tuning your skill, product, or craft is not selfish. It is stewardship. God has gifted you with your ability, mind, or craft, so when you grow, the people you serve benefit. The growth you pursue does not stay contained within you; it ripples outward. For me, the people I serve are my community and the individuals

"THE GROWTH YOU
PURSUE DOES NOT STAY
CONTAINED WITHIN YOU;
IT RIPPLES OUTWARD."

who come to me seeking healing, clarity, and emotional safety. Every time I deepen my self-awareness, strengthen my skills, expand my understanding of trauma, or continue my own healing, the quality of support I offer increases: I listen more clearly. I respond more thoughtfully. I hold space with greater steadiness and discernment.

This principle extends far beyond my work. A doctor who continues their education serves patients with greater precision. A lawyer who sharpens their expertise advocates more effectively for those they represent. A teacher who evolves in their understanding reaches students more successfully. In every profession rooted in service, development is not optional—it is ethical because doing so helps more than just the person investing in themselves. When you refine your skills, your insights, and your capacities, the people who trust you with their lives, stories, health, healing, or futures are the ones who ultimately benefit.

You are inherently valuable, and you are also responsible for cultivating that value. You can increase it by:

Investing in yourself
Aligning with the right people
Charging what reflects your worth
Loving with maturity
Serving with compassion
Continuing to grow, even when life is heavy

So, believing in your value is essential, even if it is uncomfortable at first, especially if you've spent years giving freely, overextending, or equating humility with undervaluing yourself. But honoring your value does not diminish your heart; it protects it. Because of this, you must believe that what you have to offer is adequate. That it matters. That it can help someone save time, energy, or themselves from pain. And you must believe that it is worthy of compensation (sometimes even premium compensation). There will still be moments when you give your gifts freely because that is part of who you are, and there will be moments when it is appropriate to receive in return. You have earned this season of accepting that both can coexist.

You didn't wake up where you are in life by accident. You apprenticed. You studied. You showed up when it was hard. You made shifts. You learned from failure. You allowed yourself to be taught. You stayed open. You stayed committed. Now, the work looks different, but it doesn't stop there. Value also requires continued growth, and when you walk in that truth confidently, the right opportunities begin to meet you there.

There was a point in my life when becoming valuable required an impossible choice. I earned my bachelor's degree in liberal arts because I wanted to be a schoolteacher. Teaching mattered to me. I wanted to serve, to guide, to shape lives. But to complete my teaching credential, I would have had to remain in an abusive relationship for at least another year—and that was not a cost I could pay. So, I made a decision. I chose my safety over my original plan. My teaching career paused at substitute teaching, not because I lacked ability or commitment, but because survival came first. That decision changed the trajectory of my life, not by lowering my value, but by redirecting how I would build it.

I WAS
BUILDING
WISDOM,
TURNING
LIVED
EXPERIENCE
INTO INSIGHT,
PAIN INTO
PURPOSE,
AND
EDUCATION
INTO SERVICE.

That's when I entered Corporate America and worked as an underwriter at AAA for thirteen years. During that time, I continued developing myself. I didn't abandon growth; I adapted it.

While working full-time, I earned my master's degree in human behavior. I obtained my domestic violence certification, a second certification, and my coaching certification. I pursued additional training. I opened my nonprofit. I wrote Face Fear and Live, the curriculum. All of this happened while I was still employed at AAA, providing safety and stability for my children. This is what increasing your value often looks like in real life.

Not linear.
Not glamorous.
Not free from sacrifice.
But intentional.

Every step I took was a step toward becoming more equipped both professionally and personally. I wasn't chasing titles. I was building wisdom, turning lived experience into insight, pain into purpose, and education into service. This is what I mean when I say value is cultivated. Sometimes, you don't follow the path you imagined—you follow the one that allows you to live. Value is not determined by where you start or how straight the path is. It's determined by how intentionally you grow, and if you keep investing, learning, and growing along the way, you only increase it.

SCRIPTURE FOR REFLECTION

"Do you see someone skilled in their work? They will
serve before kings; they will not serve before officials
of low rank." —Proverbs 22:29

AFFIRMATIONS

I honor the value I have cultivated.

My growth matters, and my work is meaningful.

I am worthy of full and aligned compensation for the value I provide.

I continue to grow, refine, and serve with excellence.

GENTLE REFLECTION

What skill, gift, or experience have I developed that I am
now ready to offer confidently and without apology?

THE
EXPERIENCES
THAT ONCE
CAUSED PAIN
NOW OFFER
PERSPECTIVE.
THE LESSONS
YOU LEARNED
THE HARD WAY
NOW BECOME
ROADMAPS FOR
OTHERS.

12

EDIFY

From Healing to Legacy

Edification is the natural result of healing done well. It is what happens when growth no longer ends with you and begins to serve something beyond you. It is about contribution. If everyone paid it forward, the world would be a better place. As I shared in previous chapters, although we will never truly "arrive" at the end of our healing journey, we do grow. We gain wisdom through knowledge, experience, failure, and perseverance. And that wisdom is not meant to be stored away; it is meant to be shared. This is where living outwardly becomes part of the process.

To edify means to build others up spiritually, morally, intellectually, and emotionally without ego. It means using what you've learned to strengthen others rather than measuring yourself against them. It means choosing impact over applause. It looks like creating space for others to grow, sharing resources instead of guarding them, and helping someone believe in their ability to succeed before they fully see it themselves. As you walk in your purpose, you will naturally begin thinking beyond yourself. You will recognize opportunities to mentor, guide, and encourage. You will begin noticing who needs support, not because you feel responsible for fixing them, but because you understand what it feels like to walk without guidance. Because your journey has prepared you for this. The experiences that once caused pain now offer perspective. The lessons you learned the hard way now become roadmaps for others. And when you share from a place of humility and love, the impact multiplies.

"TO EDIFY MEANS TO BUILD OTHERS UP SPIRITUALLY, MORALLY, INTELLECTUALLY, AND EMOTIONALLY WITHOUT EGO."

It is important to realize that, even with edification, you need to create an intentional balance. This process is not about pouring until you are empty; it is about pouring from overflow. And what returns to you when you live this way cannot be purchased. It fills you in a way that achievement never could. This is legacy work—not loud, not flashy. But it's powerful.

When you build others up, you honor the work you did to heal yourself, and when you walk in abundance emotionally, spiritually, or materially, edification ensures that abundance remains meaningful. Your success matters, but what you do with it matters more.

SCRIPTURE FOR REFLECTION

"Therefore, encourage one another and build each other up, just as in fact you are doing." —1 Thessalonians 5:11

AFFIRMATIONS

I use my wisdom to uplift others.
My growth creates space for others to grow.
I walk with purpose, humility, and intention.
What I pour out returns multiplied.

GENTLE REFLECTION

Who am I being invited to encourage, mentor, or build up?
And how can I do that authentically?

CONCLUSION

Heal Your Heart, Live Your Truth

When I look back at the girl I once was, the child who asked herself what she did wrong, the teenager who tried to make sense of abandonment, the woman who carried shame, anger, and fear far longer than she deserved, I meet her now with compassion instead of judgment.

So much of my life was shaped by things that hurt me—I was harmed at a young age, and I faced abandonment, betrayal, abuse, and loss. For years, I believed those moments defined me. I carried them as evidence that I was unwanted, unworthy, or somehow lacking. I allowed those experiences to become stories about me. But healing taught me something essential: Those moments were chapters, not the title of my life.

Through forgiveness, I released people who harmed me without excusing what they did. I learned that forgiveness was never for them; it was for me. Through acceptance, I learned to separate my identity from my experiences, which let me stop blaming myself for things I did not cause or deserve. I learned that bad things happen, even to good people, and those things do not determine our worth. They do not diminish our value. They do not disqualify us from love, joy, purpose, or peace. I learned to challenge the narrative I had been telling myself for years, the one that said I wasn't chosen, wasn't valued, and wasn't deserving of healthy love. I realized that the choices others made had far more to do with them than with me. And that realization changed everything. Children ask, "What is wrong with me?" Healing adults learn to ask, "How do I move forward after what I experienced?"

Through courage, I faced fears that once controlled me. Through elimination, I released people, patterns, and beliefs that no longer served me. Through freedom, I allowed myself to dream again. Through empowerment, I took responsibility for my life without taking on shame. Through affirmation and renewal, I learned to see myself clearly and realign my life with intention. Through love, inspiration, value, and edification, I learned that healing does not end with me.

Along the way, something unexpected happened. The fragmented relationship I once had with my father was mended, not perfectly, but genuinely. What grew between us was real, steady, and safe. I learned that his choices were not a reflection of my worth, but of the limitations and struggles he carried with him. Releasing that truth didn't just bring understanding; it brought closeness. Walls softened. Conversations deepened. Love became something I could feel, not just hope for. Today, our relationship is one of presence and care. I know I am loved, and in that restoration, I discovered that healing doesn't just repair what was broken; it can create something beautiful where distance once lived.

At the same time my relationship with my father was being restored, I was learning how to love and be loved by my husband, and that overlap was not simple. There were moments of uncertainty and tension, and moments when my husband wondered, who is this man stepping back into your life? Ironically, it was my husband who first created the opening, making the call, extending the invitation, and hotel arrangements to our wedding. But when that door opened, it stirred emotions neither of us fully anticipated. There was confusion, a little resentment, and fear that something sacred between us might be disrupted. Slowly, understanding took root. My husband came to see that this was not about replacing him or competing for love. It was about an inner child who needed something only her father could give—not approval, but presence. Healing that I could not manufacture on my own. What I will always honor is this: He stayed. He learned. He grew. He chose patience when it would have been easier to withdraw. He allowed me the space to heal a wound that predated him, trusting that our love was strong enough to hold it. That trust revealed itself in one of the most meaningful moments of my life. Through that season, I learned what real partnership looks like. It is not the absence of conflict, but the willingness to grow through it together.

When I married my husband, I chose to honor the journey I had lived, not the one I wished had been different.

WALLS
SOFTENED.
CONVERSATIONS
DEEPENED.
LOVE BECAME
SOMETHING
I COULD FEEL,
NOT JUST
HOPE FOR.

The first time I married, I did not ask my father to walk me down the aisle. At the time, my mother had been the only consistent presence in my life, and it felt honest to let her stand in that place. This time was different. I asked my father to walk me halfway down the aisle, and when we reached the middle, he would gently place my hand into the hand of my then, seventeen-year-old son, who would walk me the rest of the way to my husband. When that moment unfolded, I was surrounded by the most important men in my life: the father who was healing with me, the son who had grown alongside me, the uncle who remained present, and the husband who chose me fully, knowing my story. This was love: layered, unconditional, earned, and present.

Being held by my father while being chosen by my husband taught me that love does not have to compete to be secure. It can coexist, mature, and deepen. With both relationships developing honestly, I felt something I had never felt before; not fragile, not divided, but whole. I also discovered that when you heal from the inside out, you stop chasing validation and start attracting alignment. I found healthy, grounded, and mutual love, not because I finally became "enough," but because I realized I always had been.

But here is what matters most: Healing did not give me a perfect life. It gave me a free one. This twelve-step journey did not erase my past—it redeemed it. It helped me reclaim my voice, my space, and my authority over my own life. It taught me that how someone feels about me is not my responsibility, but how I feel about myself is everything.

You do not need to chase people who do not
  choose you.
You do not need to shrink to be accepted.
You do not need to tie your worth to a person,
  a role, or an outcome.

Take up space. Voice your truth. Live with intention. You get one life, and you deserve to live it fully, freely, and unapologetically.

My prayer is that this book has reminded you of something you may have forgotten: You are not broken, you are not behind, and you are not disqualified. You are healing. You are becoming. And you are capable of reclaiming your life.

SCRIPTURE FOR REFLECTION

"He restores my soul; He leads me in the paths of righteousness for His name's sake." —Psalm 23:3

AFFIRMATIONS

I am not defined by what hurt me.
I reclaim my life with courage and grace.
I honor my healing and trust my future.
I live freely, whole, and aligned.

GENTLE REFLECTION

What truth am I ready to carry forward as I continue living my life, fully and intentionally?

INTEGRATION

A Living Practice

This book was never meant to be read once and put on a shelf. It was meant to be returned to, during different seasons, in different moments, as new layers of healing emerge, and as often as necessary.

You are not expected to move through these chapters in a straight line, master one, and then permanently advance to the next. Healing doesn't work that way. Life doesn't work that way. Some chapters may resonate deeply right now, and others may not speak to you until years later. You may return when something is stirred up within you, when an old wound resurfaces, when a relationship challenges you, or when you simply feel ready to go deeper. This work is living, layered, and ongoing—not a checklist.

You don't complete forgiveness and move on forever.
You don't arrive at courage and never feel fear again.
You don't reach love and stay untouched
   by old wounds.
You revisit.
You deepen.
You circle back.

Sometimes, you start at the beginning again, wiser than before. That is growth.

You may be practicing forgiveness while learning new boundaries, choosing courage while still feeling fear, loving deeply while maintaining self-protection, or renewing your vision while revisiting old grief—all of that is okay. You may even find yourself in three chapters at the same time. That's normal. This book is not asking you to progress perfectly. It's inviting you to stay engaged with yourself.

"THIS BOOK IS NOT ASKING YOU TO PROGRESS PERFECTLY. IT'S INVITING YOU TO STAY ENGAGED WITH YOURSELF"

Here are a few ways to integrate this work into your life:

1. Read at the pace of your nervous system.
   If a chapter stirs something heavy, pause, reflect, journal, and come back when your body feels ready.
2. Let chapters meet you where you are.
   You don't have to read in order. If you need courage today, go there. If you need love, sit there.
3. Use the reflection questions as checkpoints, not assignments. You don't need perfect answers. You need honest ones.
4. Revisit chapters when life shifts.

New seasons will bring new layers. This book will feel different each time you return to it.

This work is sustained through awareness, care, and compassion. Some days you will feel grounded and clear, and other days you will feel tender and unsure. Both belong here. You are not meant to "finish" healing. You are meant to maintain a relationship with it. Just like our physical health, emotional regulation, spiritual growth, and relationships. If something from your past shows up again, it means you are being invited to respond with the wisdom you didn't have before. It means life has revealed another opportunity to apply what you've learned, choose yourself again, and respond differently. You are not starting over. You are responding from a new place.

This book is a companion, but it is not meant to replace community, support, or safe relationships. Support is part of healing—not the opposite of it. And through your strength and the encouragement of those around you, you will see just how capable you are.

YOU WILL FORGIVE AGAIN.

YOU WILL ACCEPT AGAIN.

YOU WILL COURAGEOUSLY ACT AGAIN.

YOU WILL ELIMINATE AGAIN.

YOU WILL FREE YOURSELF AGAIN.

YOU WILL EMPOWER YOURSELF AGAIN.

YOU WILL AFFIRM AGAIN.

YOU WILL RENEW AGAIN.

YOU WILL LOVE AGAIN.

YOU WILL INSPIRE AGAIN.

YOU WILL VALUE YOURSELF AGAIN.

YOU WILL EDIFY OTHERS AS YOU GO.

You are becoming. And that is the work.

With Gratitude

TO MY CHILDREN: You are the reason I began this journey. You deserved more, and in the process of fighting to give you more, I discovered that I deserved more, too. You pushed me to heal, to grow, and to become the woman and mother you needed. Everything I do is rooted in my love for you—to show you what courage, self-worth, and perseverance look like in real life. You all make life better! You all make me better!

TO MY HUSBAND: Thank you for your patience, your partnership, and your steady presence. Pursuing healing while navigating life (and health challenges) was not easy, but we did it together. Thank you for seeing me, accepting me fully, and loving me in a way that allowed me to open my heart again. The love we share is so special and something I treasure deeply. Excited to continue our healing journey together.

TO MY MOTHER: I understand more than ever the strength it took to be a single mother raising me. I see your sacrifice. I value the life you worked so hard to give me. Thank you not only for who you were then, but for who you continue to be now—my mother, my support system, and yes, my next-door neighbor. Your continued love and presence in my day-to-day work mean more to me than words can express.

TO MY GRANDMOTHER: Though you are no longer here, your influence is woven into who I am. I lived with you during the earliest years of my life, and the lessons you taught me about strength, resilience, and love continue to guide me. Your impact did not end when you left this world.

TO MY UNCLE: Thank you for being the first and most consistent male influence in my life. Your presence throughout my childhood, teenage years, and adulthood offered stability, guidance, and care that mattered more than you may ever know.

TO MY FATHER: I am grateful for our reconciliation and for the relationship we share today. Healing within a relationship that once caused me pain was not easy, but it was incredibly restorative. I now embrace the love, joy and value of being a daddy's girl—a gift I do not take lightly.

TO MY TEAM AT HEALED WOMEN HEAL: Thank you for walking alongside me in this work. The healing we offer others is only possible because of the heart, commitment, and integrity each of you brings to this mission. I am blessed to do this work with you.

AND FINALLY, TO EVERY PERSON who has contributed to my healing journey in seen and unseen ways: Thank you. This book reflects what is possible when healing is supported, shared, and honored.

About the Author

TRACY EVANSON holds a master's degree in human behavior and is a trauma-informed relationship coach, speaker, author, and the founder and executive director of Healed Women Heal, a nonprofit organization dedicated to domestic violence prevention, education, empowerment, and emotional healing. Grounded in safety, self-worth, and purpose, she has a deep commitment to helping individuals rebuild their lives.

Evanson is also the creator of Tracy's Healing Room, a coaching and healing space designed for high-achieving women who carry unseen emotional wounds. Through one-on-one coaching, sacred containers, and community collaborations, she helps clients uncover underlying patterns, strengthen boundaries, heal relational trauma, and step fully into aligned, authentic lives.

Known for her honesty, compassion, and steadfast leadership, Tracy speaks openly about her own journey through abandonment, abuse, forgiveness, healing, and renewal—believing that true inspiration comes from transparency and growth. Through her writing, coaching, and advocacy, she creates spaces where people feel seen, supported, and empowered to face fear and live fully.